# BOOK **1** ONE

# JOHN THOMPSON'S
## ADULT PIANO COURSE

ISBN 978-1-4234-0580-1

EXCLUSIVELY DISTRIBUTED BY

WILLIS MUSIC

HAL•LEONARD®
CORPORATION
7777 W. BLUEMOUND RD. P.O. BOX 13819
MILWAUKEE, WISCONSIN 53213

Visit Hal Leonard Online at
**www.halleonard.com**

# CONTENTS

# PREFACE

**Music** is composed of three equally important parts: *Melody, Harmony* and *Rhythm*.

Briefly, *Melody* is the "air" or "tune" of the piece.
    *Harmony* is the accompaniment or background that supports the melody.
    *Rhythm* is the "swing" or "lilt" of the piece as a whole.

## MELODY APPROACH

Any of the three factors (melody, harmony, rhythm) may be used effectively as an approach to the study of music, and this is a point upon which authorities differ. The author has chosen the Melody Approach for very solid—old-fashioned, if you like—but conclusive reasons!

In the first place, all music is identified by its "tune" or melody. This is equally true of a simple lullaby or a great symphony. The melody, therefore, would seem to be the very first essential.

Secondly, by using the Melody Approach the student is enabled to "make music," or in other words, play a tune, in the very first lesson. Thus interest, appreciation, and use of the ear are fostered from the very beginning. Rhythm and harmony are approached in proper order as soon as the student is able to digest them.

Music is a great art and an exact science. By using the Melody Approach, the student is led to think of music first as an art. Later, as harmony and rhythm are introduced, the student becomes acquainted with the scientific side of music study.

## IMPORTANCE OF ENSEMBLE PLAYING

The Introductory Section of this book is arranged in the form of duets. The accompaniments "dress up" the simple melodies. They also offer certain advantages of ensemble playing by which the teacher can control the tempo, influence the rhythm, and encourage tonal contrast—all of which form the basis of interpretation.

## IMPORTANCE OF FINGERING

Strict attention to correct fingering is of great importance. In fact, one can safely say that correct fingering is just as essential as correct notes in the early stages of piano playing. It will be found later that choice of fingering forms one of the basic principles of technical proficiency.

## READING DRILLS

The alert student will quickly discover that the melodies in the Introductory Section of the book can more easily be played by observing the finger signs, or even "by ear." This should *not* be discouraged; on the contrary, *anything* which tends to help the student play musically and expressively should be welcomed and encouraged.

Independence, however, is not attained until the student can **Play By Note** (or, sight-read). To develop this the student should be required to read the little tunes and melodic phrases away from the keyboard. The teacher should treat each example as a Reading Drill. This is accomplished by **clapping** and **reciting**. The student gives one clap to each count in the bar and names the notes in time to the clapping. By clapping and reciting daily, the ability to read "by note" will quickly overtake the tendency to play "by ear" or by finger numbers.

## PREPARATORY BOOK

This book is a preparatory book for piano playing. It is designed specially for the adult, and its purpose is to lead the student quickly but thoroughly through the elements of piano study. At its conclusion the student may proceed to John Thompson's *Adult Course Book 2* and continue with succeeding books in the *Modern Course for the Piano*.

*John Thompson*

# INTRODUCTORY SECTION

# THE KEYBOARD

## MIDDLE C

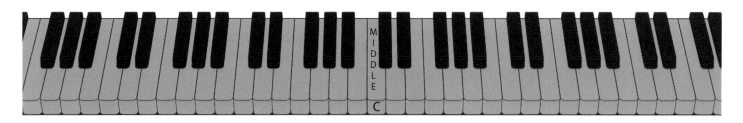

Note that the black keys on the piano are arranged in groups of two's and three's.
The C under the maker's name on your piano is known as Middle C.
Middle C is the logical key to learn first, for reasons apparent later on.
It is easily located as it lies immediately below the two-black-key group.
First, locate it on the keyboard. Then find all the other C's, using the two-black-key groups as a guide.
Next, mark the letter name of all the C's on the keyboard above.

## SHOWING A, B, C

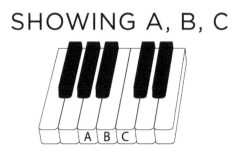

Using C as a guide, locate all the A's, B's, and C's on the keyboard. Then write the letter names of the new keys in their proper places on the keyboard at the top of the page.

## SHOWING C, D, E

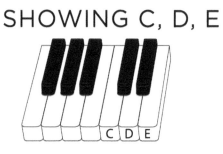

Again, using C as a guide, locate all the C's, D's, and E's on the keyboard. Then write the letter names of the new keys on the keyboard at the top of the page.

## SHOWING E, F, G

Using E as a guide, locate all the E's, F's, and G's on the keyboard and, as before, mark the new keys on the keyboard chart above.

**You have now learned and located all the white keys on the piano.**
**The names of the black keys will be presented in a later lesson.**

# ELEMENTS OF NOTATION

For the purposes of convenience, music is divided by BAR LINES into BARS.
Bars are also called "measures."

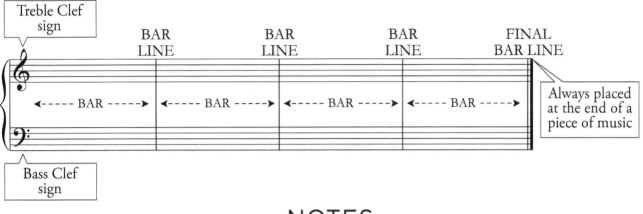

## NOTES

Solid and open-headed symbols (♩ ♪ etc.) placed on the lines or in the spaces are called NOTES.
The *position* of the notes (on various lines or spaces) indicates the piano keys to be played.
The *shape* or design of the note determines its time value.

For example:    ♩    is a QUARTER NOTE and is held for *one count*. It is also called a crotchet.

♩    is a HALF NOTE and is held for *two counts*. It is also called a minim.

o    is a WHOLE NOTE and is held for *four counts*. It is also called a semibreve.

## TIME SIGNATURES

TIME SIGNATURES, shown at the beginning of a piece, tell how to count in each bar.

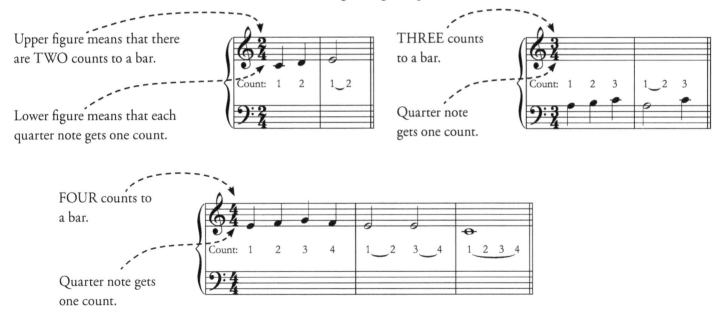

## NOTE TO TEACHERS

To facilitate reading the teacher should insist that all examples, particularly in the Introductory Section, be treated as Reading Drills. This is accomplished by having the student first announce the time signature, then follow by clapping the time (one clap to each quarter note, two claps to each half note, etc.) while reciting the letter names of the notes. This should be done *before* each example is played on the piano.

# TEACHER'S PAGE

(This page is for the teacher only.)

The Teacher's Page contains accompaniments to be played together with the student's melodies on the opposite page, thus presenting the tunes in the form of duets.

The importance of ensemble playing cannot be over-emphasized. Not only does it make the little melodies more attractive, but it enables the teacher to control the tempo, influence the rhythm (accents, etc.) and encourage tonal variation, thus adding expression from the very beginning.

# STUDENT

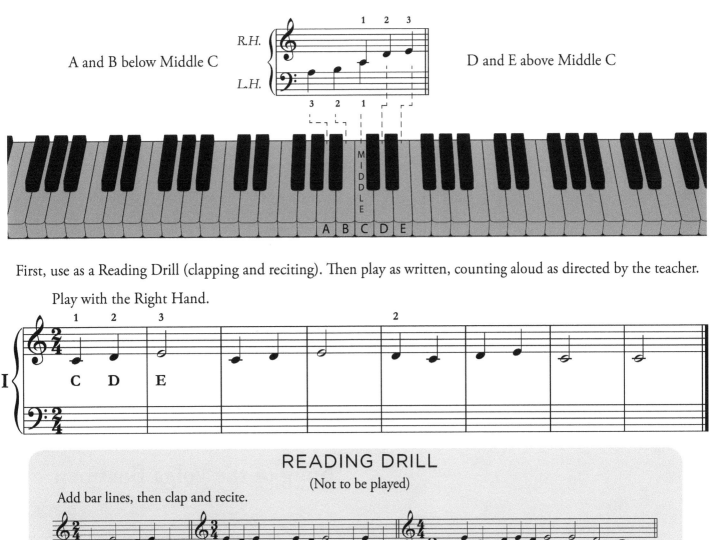

A and B below Middle C

*R.H.*

*L.H.*

D and E above Middle C

First, use as a Reading Drill (clapping and reciting). Then play as written, counting aloud as directed by the teacher.

Play with the Right Hand.

I

C  D  E

## READING DRILL
### (Not to be played)

Add bar lines, then clap and recite.

Play with the Left Hand.

II

C  B  A

## READING DRILL
### (Not to be played)

Add bar lines, then clap and recite.

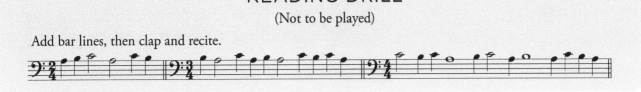

*Right Hand*

III

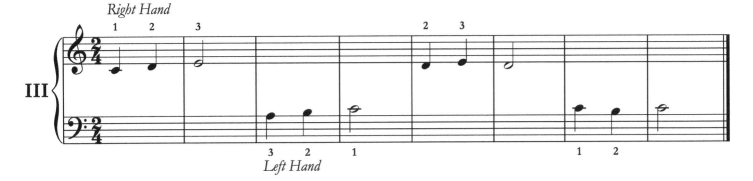

*Left Hand*

# TEACHER

At this point, explain the meaning and importance of RHYTHM, ACCENTS, and TEMPO.

RHYTHM is often called the *Soul of Music*. The first step in setting the rhythm is by means of the accent.

ACCENT is a special emphasis placed upon certain beats in a bar—at present on the first beat.

TEMPO means time. A steady, even tempo is necessary to preserve the rhythmical "swing." This means there will be no time to stop and hunt for notes, keys, or fingers. After a piece has been learned it should be reviewed until it can be played fluently and easily, without stops or hesitation.

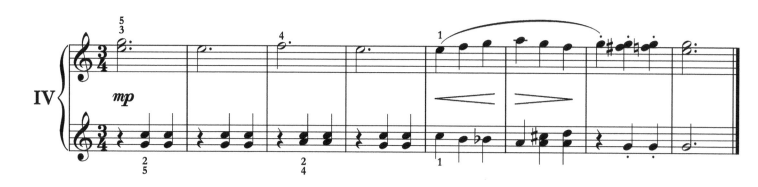

## Song of the Volga Boatmen

Russian Folk Song

### TEACHER'S NOTE

Be insistent in the matter of *clapping* and *reciting*. It is the only way to ensure *playing by note*.

Now that the student has learned what *accent* means, it would be a good plan to include it in the Reading Drills by requiring an accented clap on the first beat of each bar while reciting the letter names of the notes.

## Chimes

# STUDENT

New notes
F and G below Middle C
(L.H. Group)

New notes
F and G above Middle C
(R.H. Group)

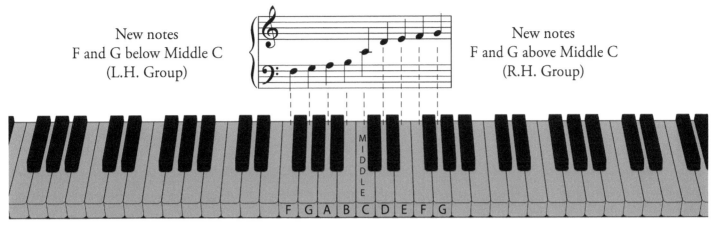

## THE DOTTED HALF NOTE

A dot after a note increases its time value by one half.
A dotted half note therefore gets three counts.

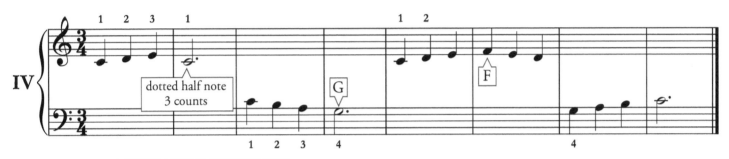

### REST SIGNS

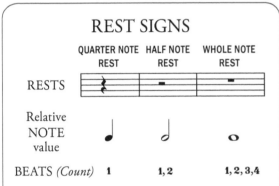

| | QUARTER NOTE REST | HALF NOTE REST | WHOLE NOTE REST |
|---|---|---|---|
| RESTS | 𝄽 | ▬ | ▬ |
| Relative NOTE value | ♩ | 𝅗𝅥 | 𝅝 |
| BEATS (Count) | 1 | 1, 2 | 1, 2, 3, 4 |

The REST sign in music notation is a sign of silence. All notes have their equivalents in rest signs. Each beat of a bar must be accounted for either in notes or rests. The whole note rest is used to indicate a full bar's silence regardless of the number of beats it contains.

## Song of the Volga Boatmen

Russian Folk Song

## Chimes

# TEACHER

## TEACHER'S NOTE

Since the student encounters the sharp sign for the first time in Example X, it would be well at this point to teach the names of the five black keys, using the sharp names only (C♯ D♯ F♯ G♯ A♯). The flat names will be taken up later.

# STUDENT

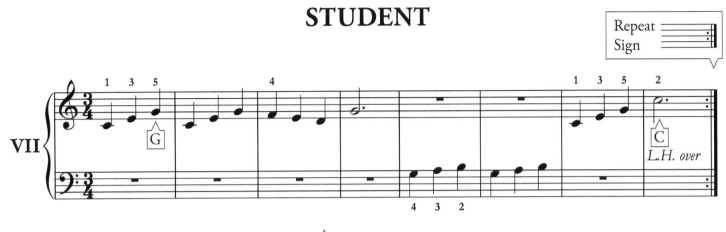

The time value of an eighth note ♪ is half as long as that of a quarter note.

Play TWO eighth notes ♫ to ONE count.

The sign ♯ is called a sharp. In the following example, the sharp indicates that the black key above (to the right of) F should be played.

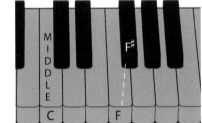

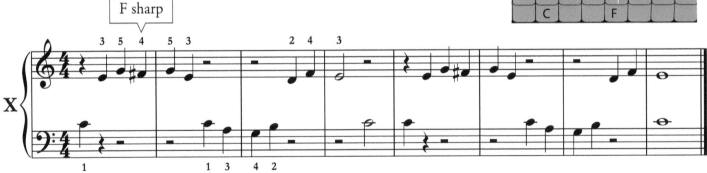

## READING DRILL
(Not to be played)

Clap and recite.

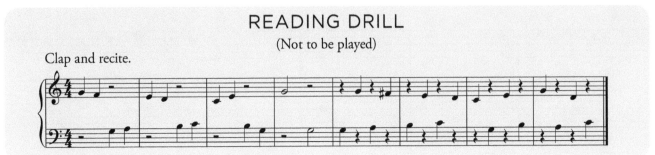

# TEACHER

## Petite Valse

## The Bee

## Blue Bells of Scotland

Old Scottish Air

# STUDENT

## Petite Valse

When the sharp sign (♯) is placed here, it becomes the KEY SIGNATURE. In this piece all the F's must be sharp.

The TIE indicates that the second note is to be held for its full value without being struck.

## The Bee

A sharp

## Blue Bells of Scotland

Old Scottish Air

NOTE: This piece begins on the fourth beat.

Repeat Sign

C sharp

# TEACHER

No book in itself can take the place of the teacher. This is particularly true in teaching such matters as hand posture and general technique.

In the early examples the wise teacher is not too insistent about technical principles. Rather, every effort is made to have the student *think* and *feel* musically, even if it is at the expense of ideal playing conditions.

Perhaps the real test of a teacher is to know how lenient to be without establishing bad habits. Start with the Finger Drill on page 15; however, attention should be given to hand position, finger curve, correct action, etc.

This procedure is left entirely to the teacher since each will have individual ideas of presenting technique, and they will vary somewhat with each student.

## TEACHER'S NOTE

Teach the flat names of the five black keys (D♭ E♭ G♭ A♭ B♭). Show how the *natural* sign cancels sharps and flats.

## Down South
(Strain from "Dixie")

## Comin' Round the Mountain

**As lively as possible**

Southern Mountain Song

# STUDENT

REATING AND FINGER DRILL

The FLAT sign = ♭
The black key below (to the left of) A.

The NATURAL sign = ♮
cancels all previous sharps or flats.

## Down South

F sharp

F natural

A flat

In this piece all B's must be flat.

## Comin' Round the Mountain

Southern Mountain Song

**As lively as possible**

*Repeat ad lib.*

L.H.

L.H.

# TEACHER

## Home on the Range

Cowboy Ballad

**Slowly, with much expression**

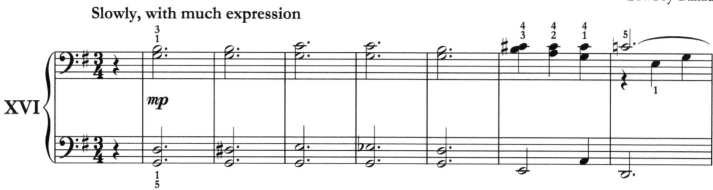

# STUDENT

# STUDENT

## SEVEN READING DRILLS

Draw bar lines as indicated by the time signatures. Then clap the rhythm and recite the letter names of the notes.

(Not to be played)

## TEACHER'S NOTE

The above drills contain all the notes, rests, time values, and time signatures learned so far. If the student is able to clap and recite each drill with accuracy and a fair amount of fluency, they are ready to proceed with the next section of the book. Otherwise, the Introductory Section should be reviewed as often as necessary until the ability to read well is assured.

# INTRODUCTORY SECTION REVIEW

If the Introductory Section has been carefully studied, the student is now familiar with the following:

**Keyboard**—The names of all keys, black and white, on the keyboard.

**Bars and Bar lines**—What they are and what they mean.

**Treble and Bass Clef Signs**—Their effect on the lines and spaces of the staff.

**Time Values**—The Whole Note, Half Note, Dotted Half Note, Quarter Note, Eighth Note and their equivalents in Rests.

**Time Signatures**       $\frac{2}{4}$   $\frac{3}{4}$   $\frac{4}{4}$

**Notes in the Treble**

**Notes in the Bass**

**Accidentals**—Sharp ($\sharp$), Flat ($\flat$), and Natural ($\natural$) signs.

**The Tie**

**The Repeat Sign**

**Reading**—By consistent practice of **clapping** and **reciting**, the student should have acquired facility in reading the notes learned so far.

**Melody** and **Rhythm**—The musical experiences gained by this time have developed a sense of rhythm and melodic flow.

**Harmony**—Hearing the teacher's accompaniments will instill a "listening acquaintance" with harmony.

In short, the student is now fully prepared to enter the Main Section of the book. From this point on, the hands will be required to play together. The examples will expand gradually in all directions, making more demands both musically and technically.

## TEACHER'S NOTE

Quite often, in the case of students who have had preliminary training in music, it will be unnecessary to go through the Introductory Section. This is solely for the teacher to decide.

# JOHN THOMPSON'S
# ADULT PIANO COURSE

## MAIN SECTION

## HOW TO STUDY

One of the most important aids to piano study is that of knowing *how* to practice.
Mastery is not gained through monotonous repetition.
*"Practice makes perfect"* is an old saw which has proven to be a fallacy. To be effective it would have to be qualified as follows: *"(Correct) practice (if repeated often enough) makes perfect."*

## IMPORTANCE OF ACCURACY

The importance of accuracy, therefore, becomes at once apparent.
Never play anything faster than it can be played correctly.
Each time a mistake is made, some of the previous practice is undone.
The wise student naturally studies first each hand separately—later putting the hands together.

## IMPORTANCE OF REVIEW

While studying the new lesson, don't overlook the importance of reviewing the work covered in previous lessons. It is in repeating examples *after they are learned* that the greatest benefits are derived, especially those having to do with the technique of piano playing.

## FINGER DRILLS

Don't neglect the Finger Drills. They are designed to develop independence, strength, and fluency of finger action. Daily repetition of the drills will provide a "short-cut" to piano technique.

## READING

If there is the slightest doubt about the student's ability to read the notes fluently, the practice of **clapping** and **reciting** should be continued. In general, practice each hand separately from this point on.

# THE PHRASE

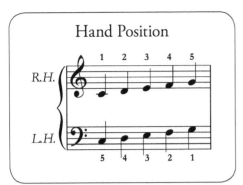

Music, like language, is expressed in phrases. Single notes by themselves mean nothing. Only when the notes are arranged into musical phrases do they take on a definite meaning. Learn to think of your music *phrase by phrase*. Notice how the first phrase is answered by the second phrase in each of the following examples.

## MUSICAL FORM

Because it is built up of many well-ordered patterns, music is often compared to architecture. We have in music: *Melody Patterns, Rhythmical Patterns, Harmony Patterns*, and, in piano music, *Finger Patterns*. The ability to recognize patterns is very important. It makes for easier sight reading, quicker memorizing, and more intelligent interpretation.

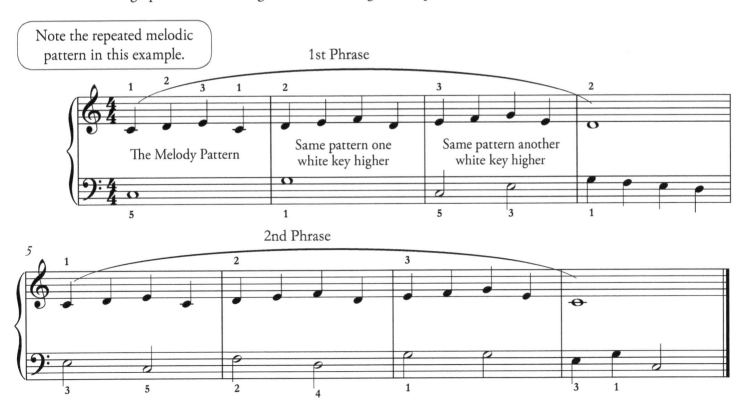

# FINGER DRILL

## TONAL SHADING

"Contrast is the first law of Art." One of the first steps in securing contrast is by means of tonal shading. Be sure to learn the meaning of the expression marks indicated in the following piece. They are explained at the bottom of the next page.

## Swans on the Lake

John Thompson

**Moderato**

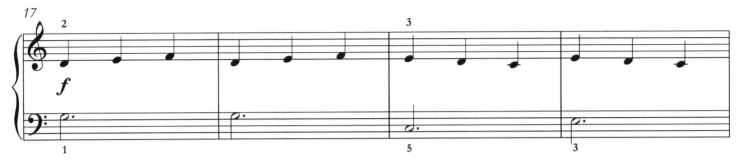

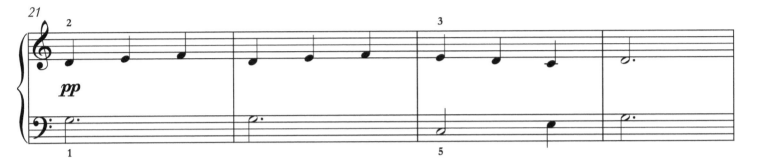

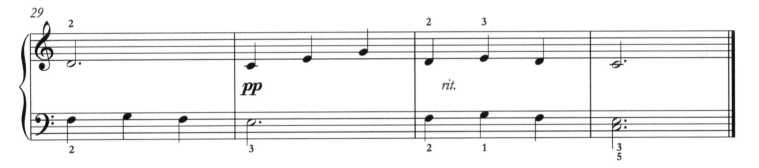

**The Meaning of the Expression Marks used in this Piece**

MODERATO—At a moderate speed.

LEGATO—Bound together, smoothly connected.

*mf* = MEZZO FORTE—Moderately loud.

*p* = PIANO—Softly.

*f* = FORTE—Loud.

*pp* = PIANISSIMO—Very soft.

*mp* = MEZZO PIANO—Moderately soft.

*rit.* = RITARDANDO—Gradual slowing up of tempo.

# HALF STEPS

A HALF STEP is the distance between any key and the next nearest key.

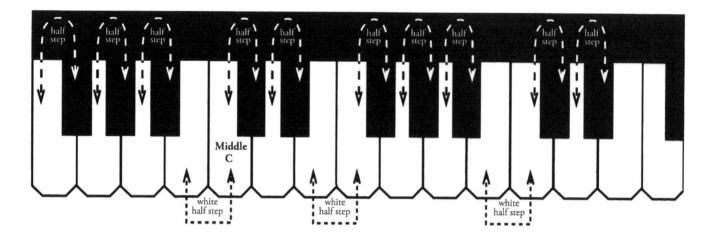

We find most of the HALF STEPS are from a WHITE to a BLACK key. There are, however, TWO white half steps—one between B and C and the other between E and F. Study them on this chart and locate them on the keyboard of your piano until they can be quickly recognized.

# WHOLE STEPS

A WHOLE STEP is twice the distance of a half step. Therefore, there will always be ONE key—either black or white—lying between.

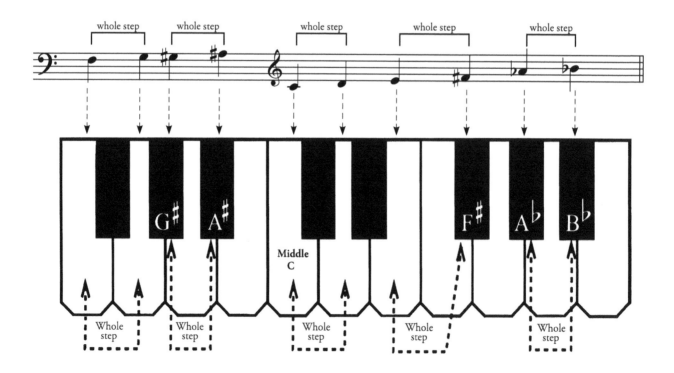

# WHOLE AND HALF STEPS

Write the name of each INTERVAL (distance) below the following examples.

*Ex.* From *F* to *G* is a *whole step*

From ___ to ___ is a

From ___ to ___ is a

From ___ to ___ is a

From ___ to ___ is a

From ___ to ___ is a

From ___ to ___ is a

Hand Position

R.H.

L.H.

NOTE:
Both hands in
Treble Clef.

## Stepping Stones

John Thompson

**Moderato**

The melody in the right hand of "Stepping Stones" passes through 16 half steps of which 8 are *white key* half steps. Can you locate all of them?

# DRILL FOR THE LEFT HAND
## Leger Lines

# In the Swing

John Thompson

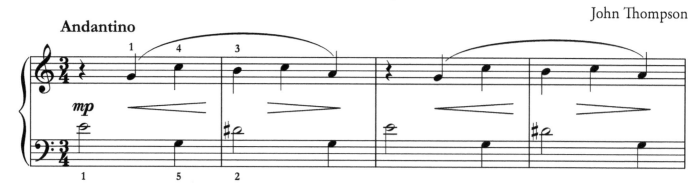

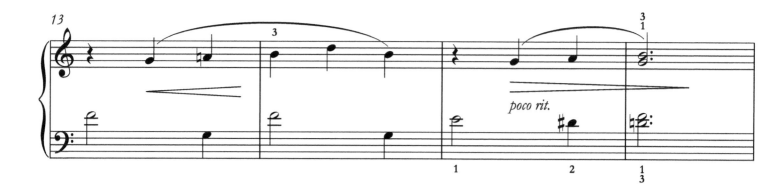

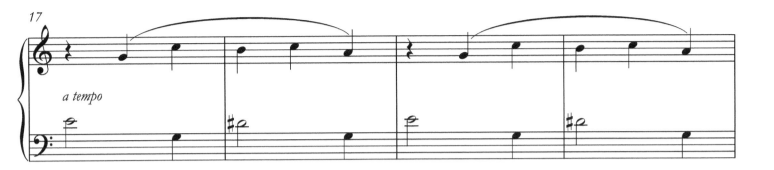

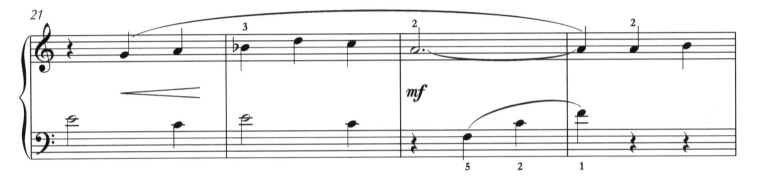

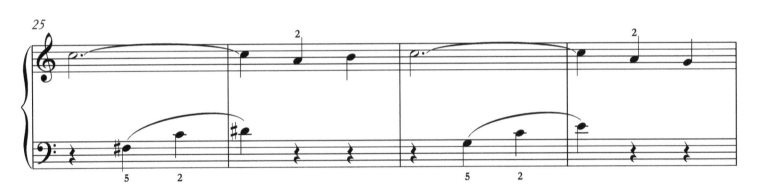

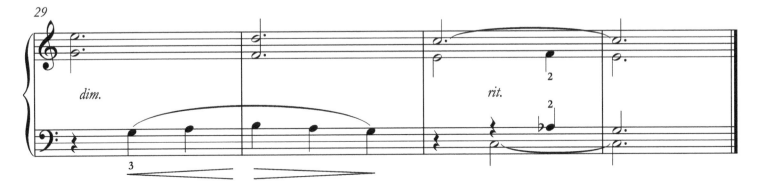

# PHRASING

What bowing is to the violinist, breathing to the singer, enunciation to the speaker, **phrasing** is to the pianist.

A simple, two-note phrase properly executed, not only breathes and is separated from the next phrase, but produces a tonal inflection that adds to the beauty and interpretation of the music.

The proper attack for a two-note phrase is very easy to accomplish. Simply remember the words, *DROP-ROLL*, and the effect comes naturally. In the following example, play the first note of each phrase with a gentle drop of the arm. The second note is played with a rolling motion of the arm and hand in an inward and upward movement, using no finger action and releasing the note on the upward roll.

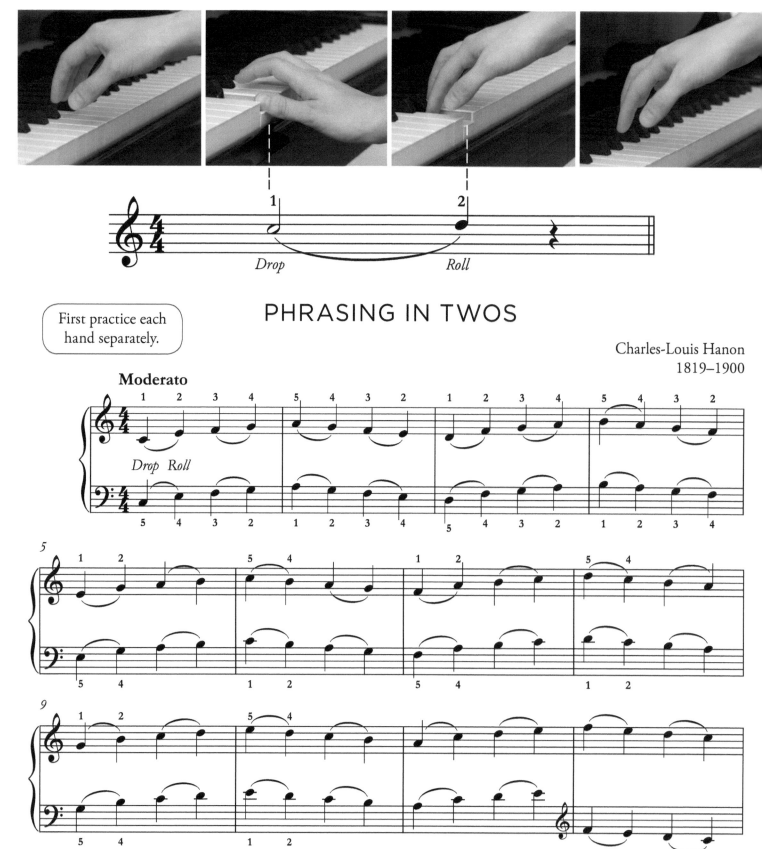

First practice each hand separately.

# PHRASING IN TWOS

Charles-Louis Hanon
1819–1900

**Moderato**

This study (and all other Hanon Studies in this book) should be reviewed daily.

In this piece observe the following:

1. The melody lies in the left hand.
2. Melody progresses by half steps and whole steps. Analyze.
3. The accompaniment in the right hand is a series of two-note phrases. Use *Drop-Roll*.

# Swaying Silver Birches

(Petite Valse)

John Thompson

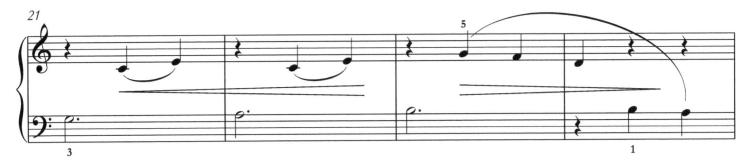

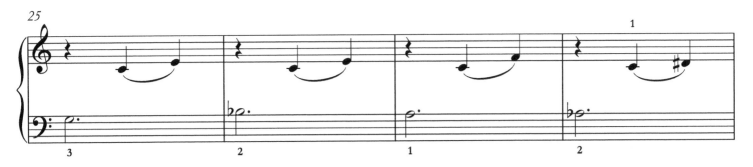

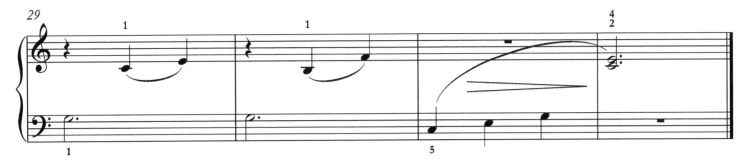

## PHRASING IN FOURS

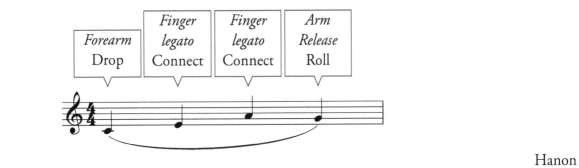

Hanon

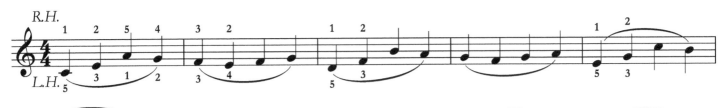

# DANCE FORMS

In music, RHYTHM is always uppermost. This is particularly true when playing *dance forms*. It is the rhythm that gives the dance its distinctive character. In a Dutch dance the accent is a very heavy one. The first beat is usually phrased into the second and tossed off sharply. Imagine Dutch children dancing in their wooden shoes and see if you can evoke a land of canals and tulips.

## Dutch Dance

John Thompson

## REVIEW

The Hanon studies on pages 28 and 31 should be reviewed daily.

# THE MAJOR SCALE

A SCALE is a succession of eight notes bearing letter names in alphabetical order, the last note having the same letter name as the first. The figures 1, 2, 3, 4, 5, 6, 7, 8 are called the degrees of the scale.

A MAJOR SCALE is a succession of WHOLE STEPS and HALF STEPS.
The half steps occur between 3 and 4 and between 7 and 8 as follows:

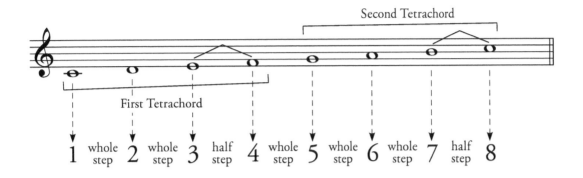

The above chart shows how a MAJOR SCALE is composed of TWO TETRACHORDS, each tetrachord separated by a WHOLE STEP.

## Scale of C Major

Play the scale of C MAJOR as follows, using the fingers indicated.

## Scale of G Major

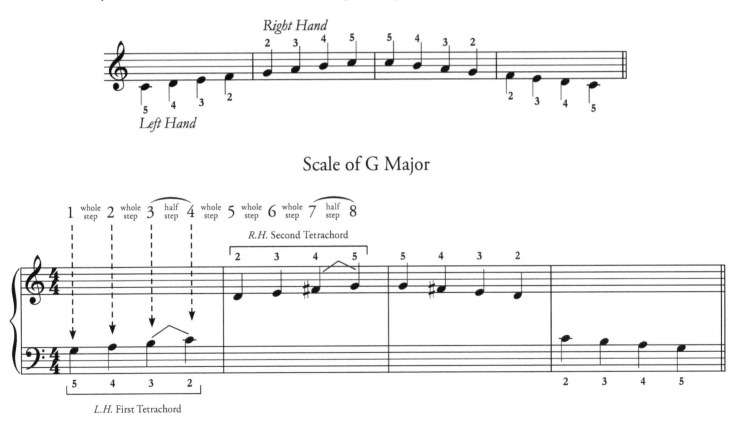

**Note to Teachers:** During the progress in this book, it is advisable to adhere to the above form—the scale divided between the hands—until scale construction in all keys has been thoroughly mastered. This obviates the necessity of passing the thumb under and the hand over—a procedure which is comprehensively taken up and illustrated by examples in Book 2.

# ETUDE
## Scale of C Major (Ascending)

# Church Bells
## Scale of C Major (Descending)

John Thompson

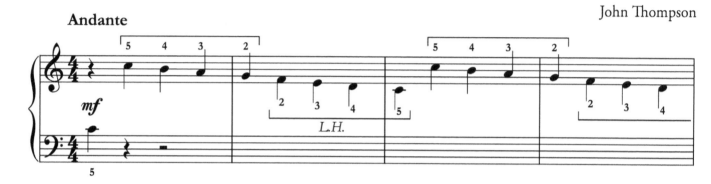

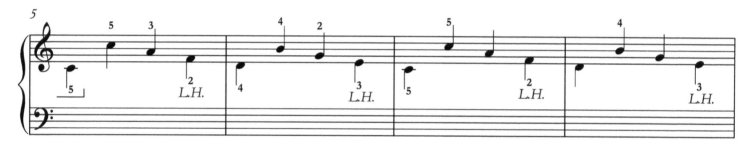

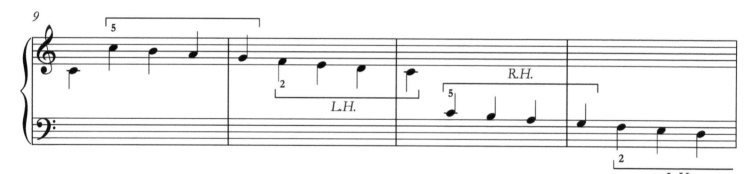

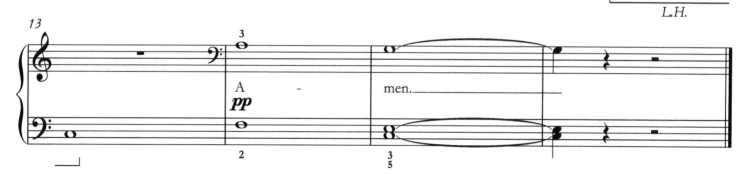

# ETUDE
## Scale of G Major

FIRST AND SECOND ENDINGS
After the repetition, do not play the
First Ending, but skip instead to the Second Ending

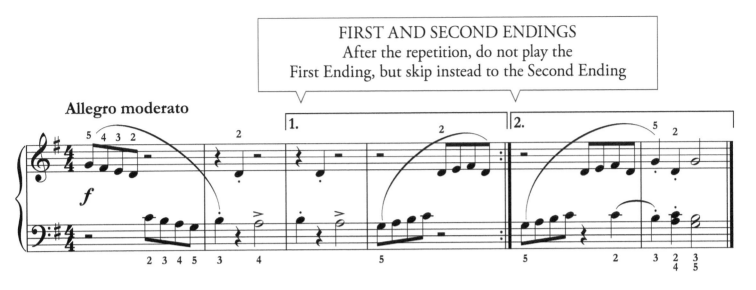

**Allegro moderato**

# Lullaby
## (Intermezzo, Op. 117, No. 1)
### Showing the Scale used as Melody

Johannes Brahms
1833–1897

**Andante moderato**

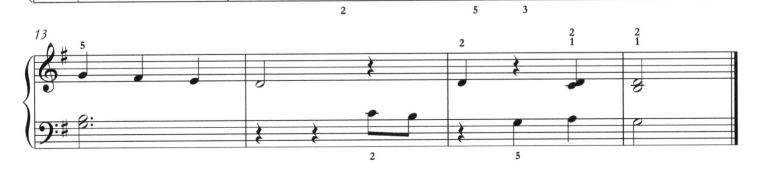

# CHORD BUILDING

A CHORD is a group of three or more notes.

If we take the 1st, 3rd and 5th notes of the scale of C Major:

And sound them together thus:

G is the **5th**.
We have played the C Major TRIAD of which E is the **3rd**.
C is the **root**.

Triads can be built upon all degrees of the scale. Every triad is named for its root.

Example:

G Major triad    F Major triad

# CHORD INVERSIONS

We have learned that a triad contains a root, a 3rd and a 5th. The order of these notes may change *without changing the name of the chord.*

When the lowest note is the root, the triad is in the ROOT POSITION.
When the lowest note is *not* the root, the triad is said to be INVERTED.

# C MAJOR TRIAD

Example:

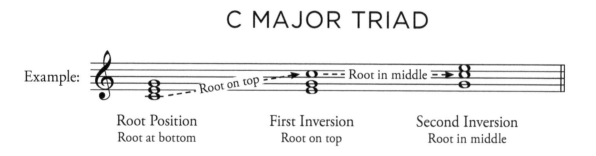

Root Position    First Inversion    Second Inversion
Root at bottom    Root on top    Root in middle

### BROKEN CHORD or ARPEGGIO

When the notes of a chord are separated and played in the following manner, it is known as a **broken chord** or **arpeggio**.

ARPEGGIO is an Italian word meaning *in the style of a harp.*

# ARPEGGIO DRILL

Play all notes under this sign
one octave higher than written.

Moderato

Circle all
broken chords.

# ETUDE
## Broken Chords

Moderato

# DRILL
## F Major Scale and Arpeggio

Circle all broken chords.

# ETUDE
## Chords and Broken Chords

# Marche Slav

Pyotr Ilyich Tchaikovsky
1840–1893

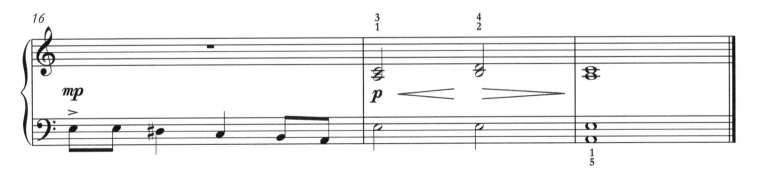

While the actual study of minor scales and modes is not presented until the student has reached Book 2, a few examples in minor mode are included in this book. They provide additional study in ear training and offer material for teachers who prefer to teach minor scales early. The above example is in the key of A Minor.

# FINGER LEGATO

Raise and drop the fingers with military precision. Keep the hand and arm perfectly quiet.

This touch develops independence and strength in the fingers, and produces clean, articulated passage playing.

Hanon

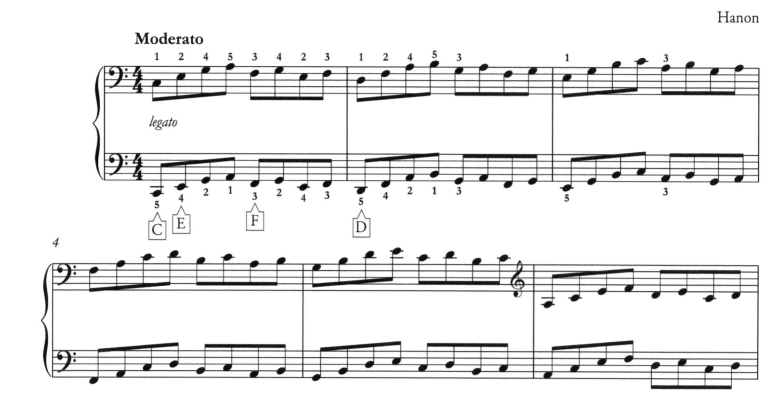

# DRILL
## Broken Chord with Inversions

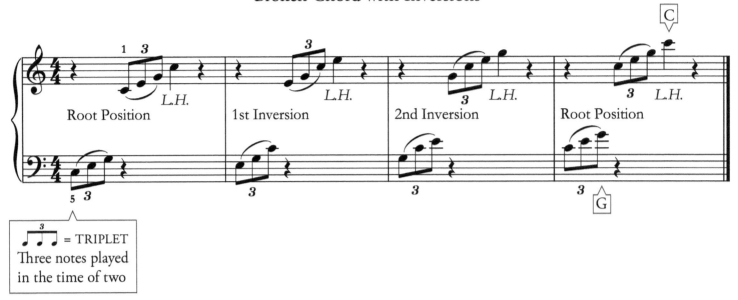

Root Position      L.H.          1st Inversion      L.H.          2nd Inversion      L.H.          Root Position      L.H.

= TRIPLET
Three notes played
in the time of two

# Forest Dawn

John Thompson

**Moderato**

FIRST THEME

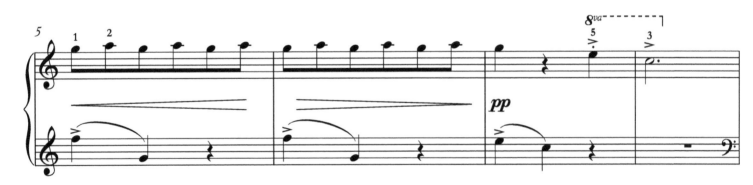

Fine

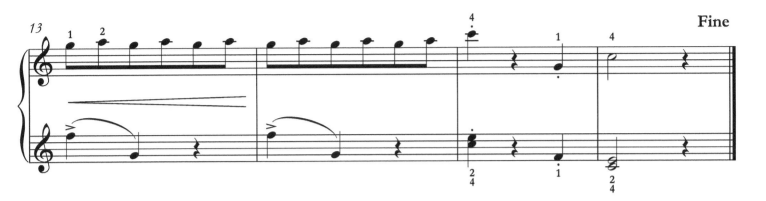

## SECOND THEME

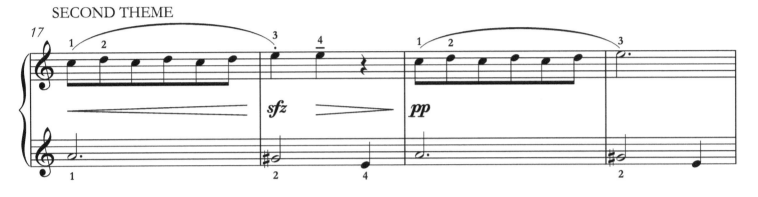

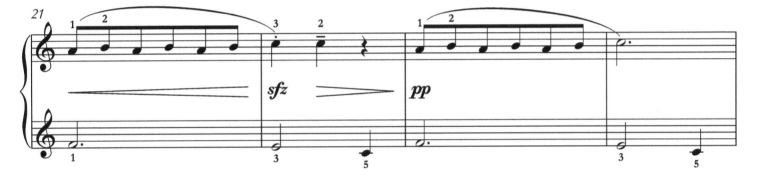

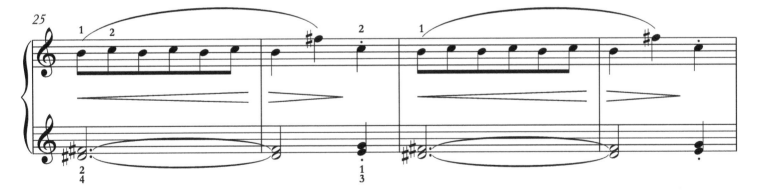

D.C. al Fine

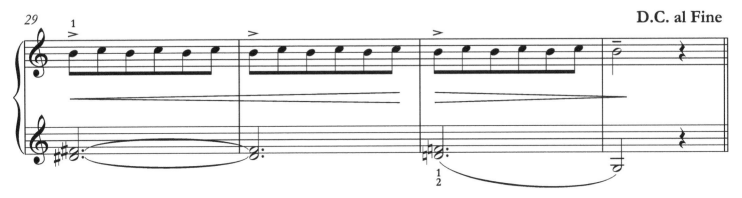

44

# DRILL
## D Major Scale and Arpeggio

**Moderato**

*mf*

L.H.
over
$8^{va-}$⌐

$8^{va-}$⌐ = Play all the notes under this sign one octave higher than written.

Be sure to observe phrasing.

# Lightly Row

Traditional Melody

**Moderato**

*mp*

*mp*

*p*

*p*

*mp*

# DRILL
## A Major Scale and Arpeggio

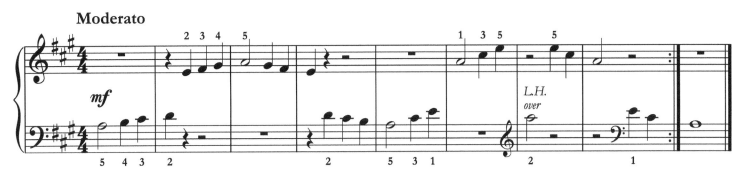

# Air
## (from Sonata in A Major)

Wolfgang Amadeus Mozart
1756–1791

DOTTED QUARTER NOTE
♩. equals 1½ counts

# ETUDE

Sharp rhythm.
Smooth finger legato.
Observe phrasing.

John Thompson

# Moccasin Dance

John Thompson

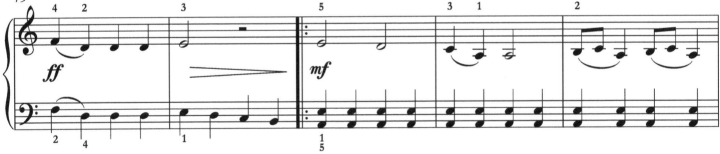

Another example in the minor mode: "Moccasin Dance" is in the key of A Minor.

# ETUDE
## F Major Scale and Chord Figures

# The Dancing Lesson
## A Study in Leger Lines

John Thompson

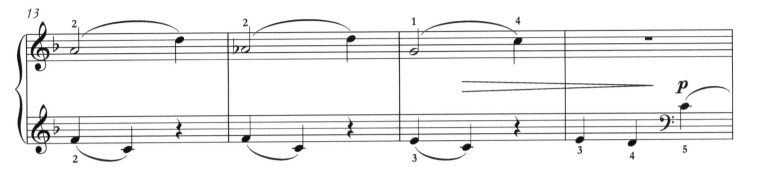

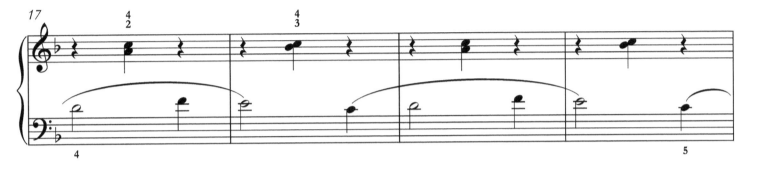

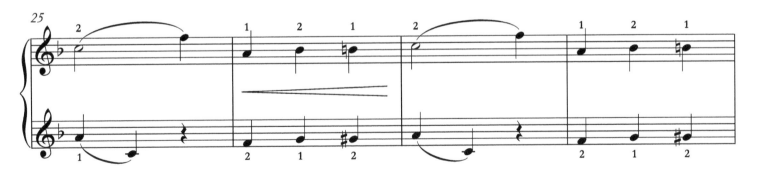

# WRIST STACCATO

In this attack the wrist acts as a hinge. No finger action is used and the hand bounces up and down.

Be sure the effort is given in the motion toward the keys and *not* on the up-stroke.

A stiff wrist is usually the result of raising the hand too high (on the up-stroke). This touch produces a crisp, percussive staccato.

PREPARATION          ATTACK          RELEASE

First practice each
hand separately.

Hanon

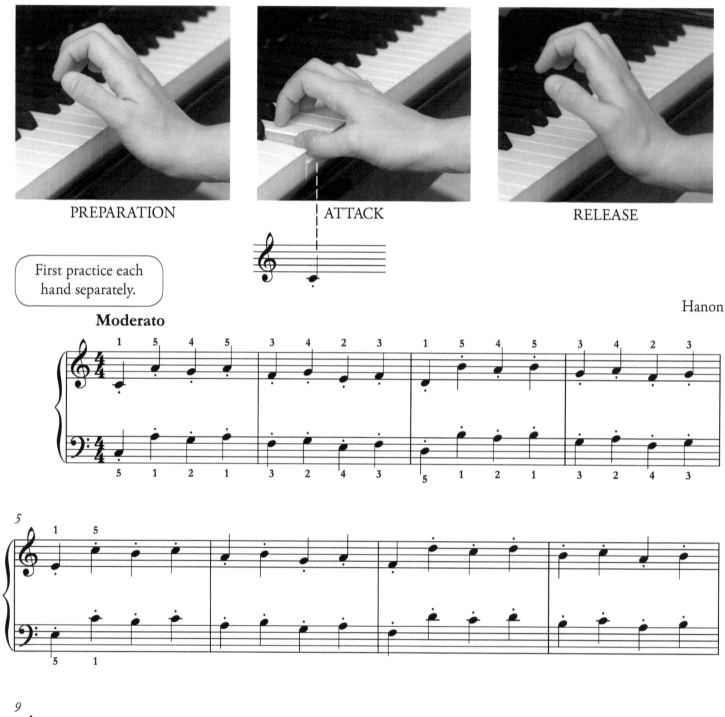

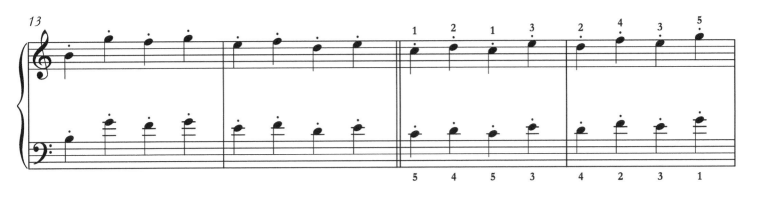

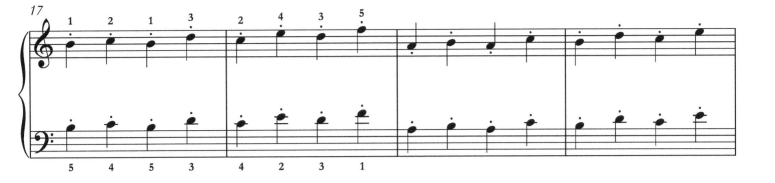

# ETUDE
## Wrist Staccato

eighth note rest

# The Woodpecker
## Wrist Staccato

John Thompson

# $\frac{6}{8}$ TIME

In $\frac{6}{8}$ time there are SIX counts to the bar and *an eighth note gets one count.* There are two accents to the bar, the primary accent falling on the FIRST count and the secondary accent on the FOURTH count.

Time Values in $\frac{6}{8}$ Time

♪ = One count

♩ = Two counts     ♩ = Four counts

♩. = Three counts     ♩. = Six counts

# Drink to Me Only with Thine Eyes

Old English Air

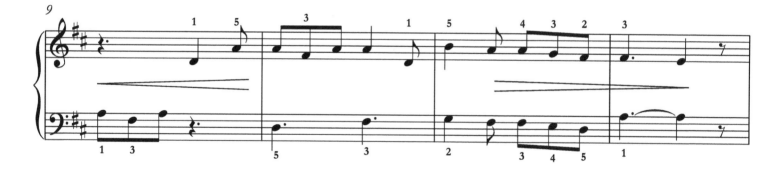

# ETUDE
## Staccato and Legato

# The Cuckoo Clock
## Two-note Phrasing

John Thompson

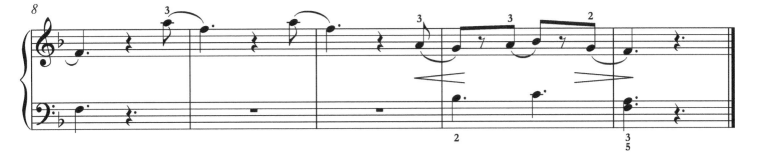

# ETUDE
## Wrist Staccato in Double Notes

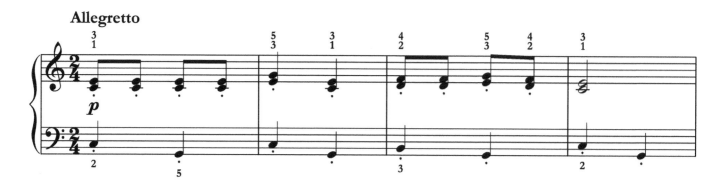

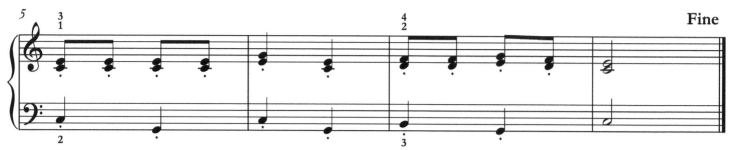

# Valse

John Thompson

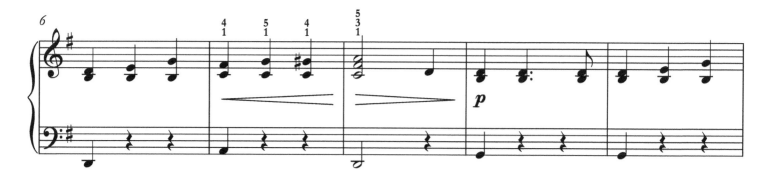

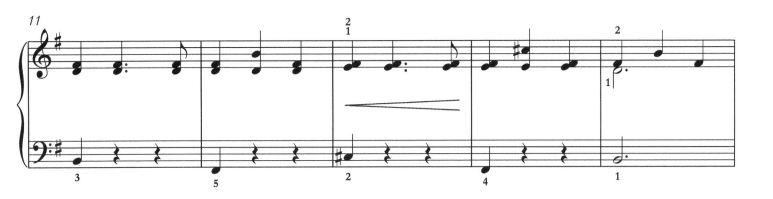

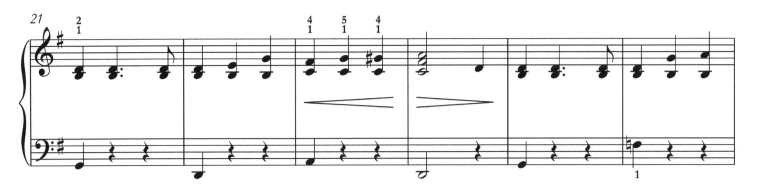

# DRILL
## B-flat Major Scale and Arpeggio

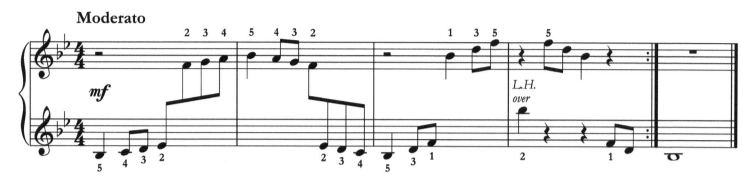

A *nocturne* is a night song. It is a composition written in lyric style suggesting the peace of evening. In the following example the melody should be played with a smooth, singing tone. Make the phrases "breathe" on the second and fourth lines, and play the left hand throughout with a light touch so as not to obscure the right-hand melody.

# Nocturne

John Thompson

# DRILL

Transpose the drill on the previous page to the key of E-flat Major.

🎵 = Pause or fermata

# Etude in E-flat Major

John Thompson

# ETUDE
## On an Irish Green

Finger Legato, Phrasing
and Melody Playing

Emphasize the drone
effect of the bass in imitation
of Irish bagpipes.

John Thompson

**Sharp and rhythmic**

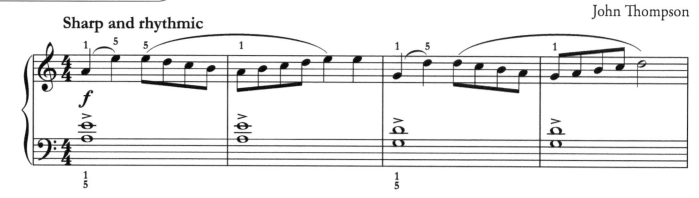

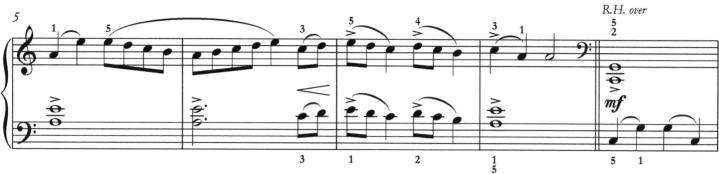

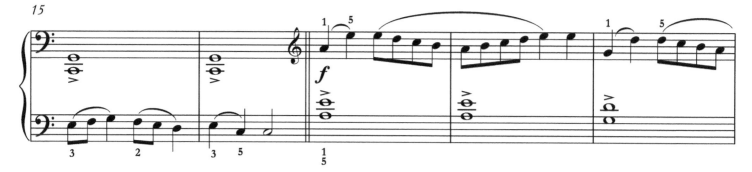

# Silent Night

Be careful of fingering.

Franz Grüber

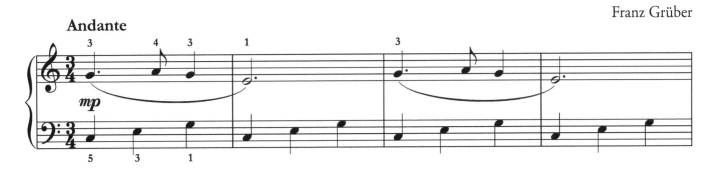

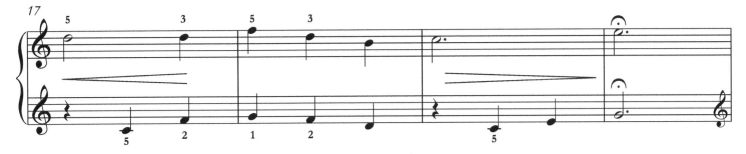

# ETUDE

# Rain Dance

### For Left Hand Alone

John Thompson

> A left-hand study.
> Make distinction between
> *staccato* and *sostenuto*.

**Expressively**

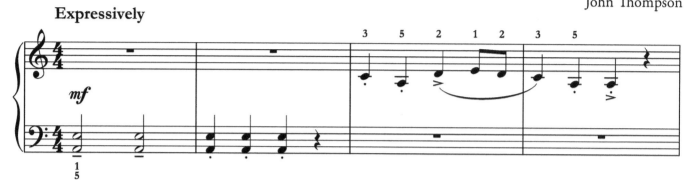

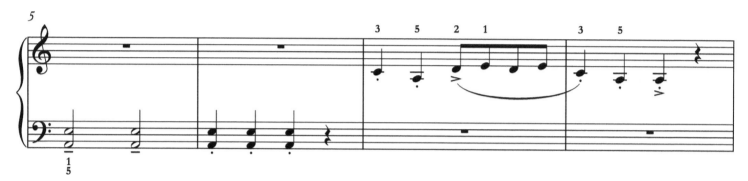

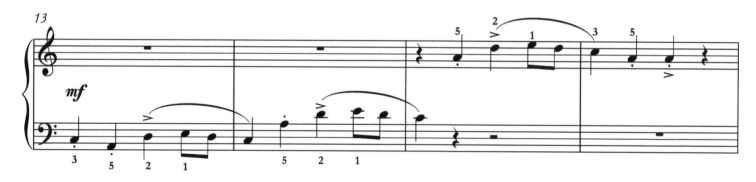

# SYNCOPATION

Tying over the last half of the first beat into the first half of the second beat results in a rhythmic effect known as SYNCOPATION. The effect will be aided by giving a slight emphasis to the notes marked: ♪

## A Spanish Fiesta

John Thompson

# DRILL
### E Major Scale and Arpeggio

**Moderato**

The left-hand part represents the drone of the bass viols which were often used to make the music to which the peasants danced on the village green.

## Peasant Dance

John Thompson

**Rhythmically**

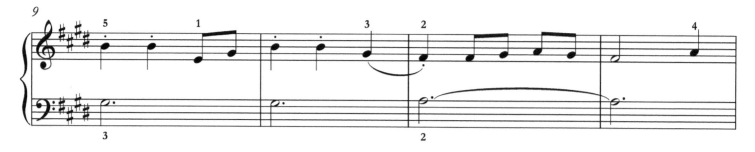

# ETUDE

## The Lonesome Pine

### Extended Broken Chords

John Thompson

Keep an unbroken legato
and play with as much
expression as possible.

**Molto legato**

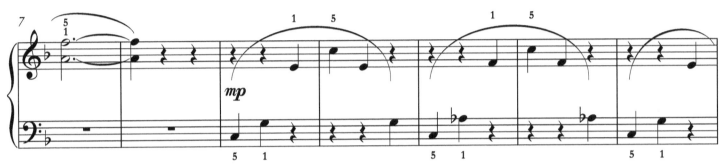

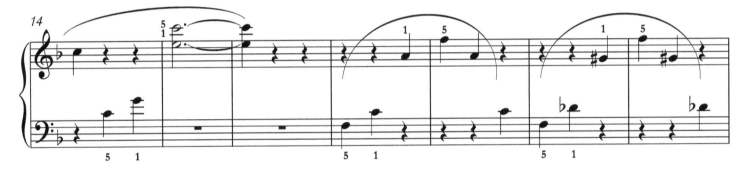

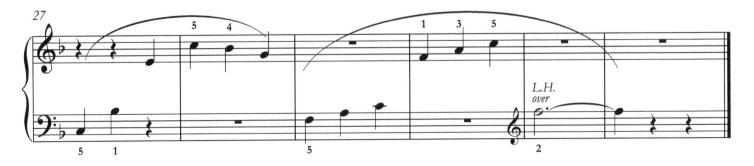

# NEW FORM OF THE BROKEN CHORD

This example employs another form of the broken chord used as accompaniment.

The HARMONY PATTERNS should be practiced first like this:

Then in broken form like this:

# Long, Long Ago

Thomas H. Bayly
1797–1839

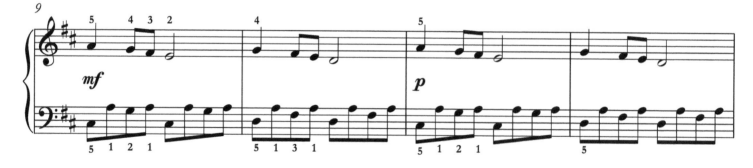

# FOREARM STACCATO

For this touch the elbow is the hinge. When in mid-air the hand hangs loosely from the wrist. At the moment of impact with the keys, the wrist drops to normal (level) position.

This touch makes more use of the weight principle, rather than wrist staccato, and the result is a staccato with more depth of tone. It is used mostly for chords and octaves.

PREPARATION

ATTACK

RELEASE

First practice each hand separately.

Hanon

# Twilight Song

## Forearm Chord Playing

John Thompson

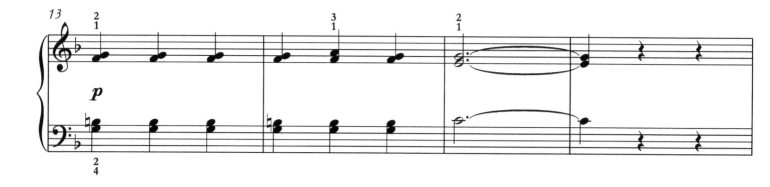

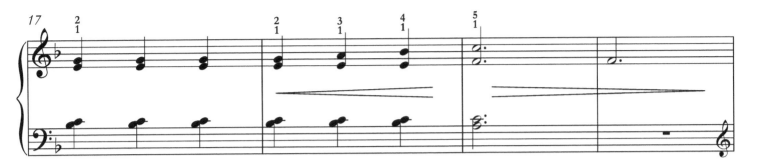

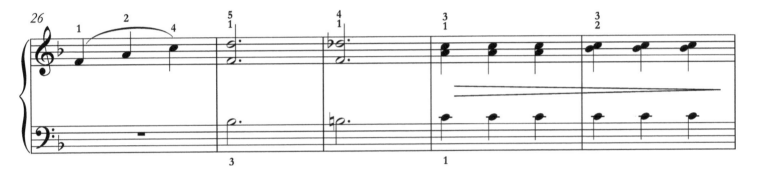

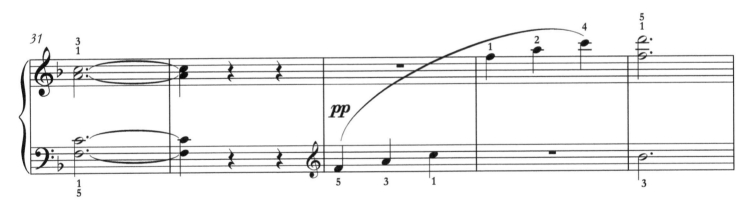

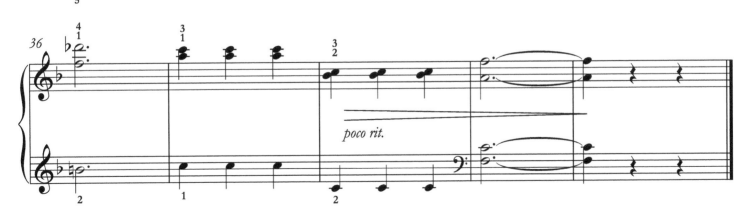

# DRILL
## A-flat Major Scale and Arpeggio

**Moderato**

## To a Skyscraper

John Thompson

**Andante**

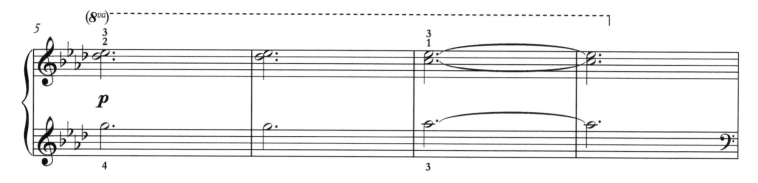

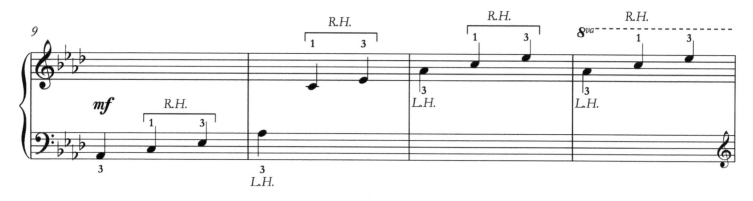

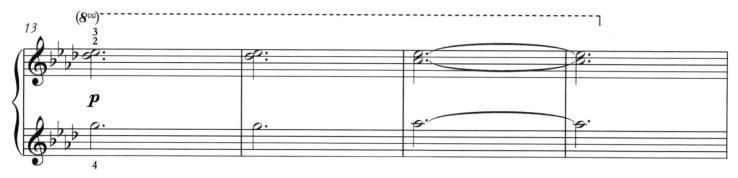

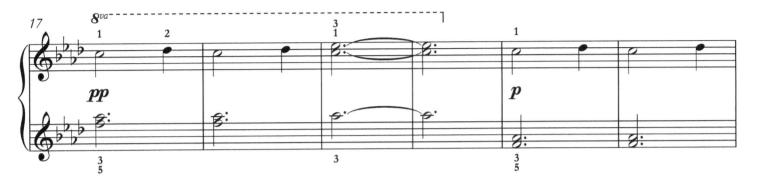

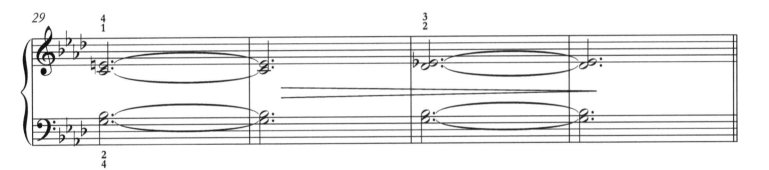

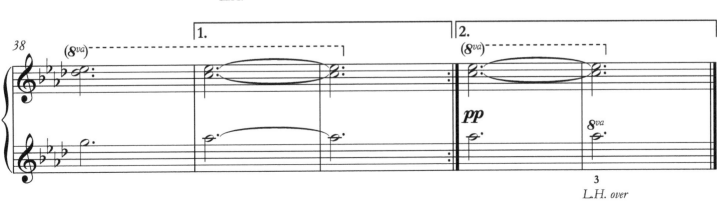

# Air

## from "New World" Symphony (No. 9)

Antonín Dvořák
1841–1904

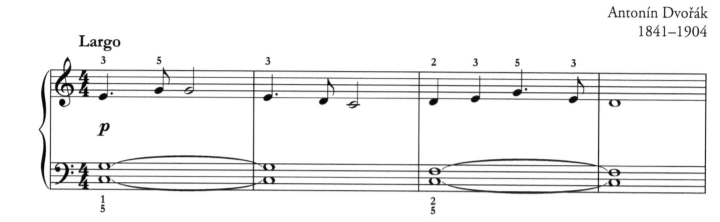

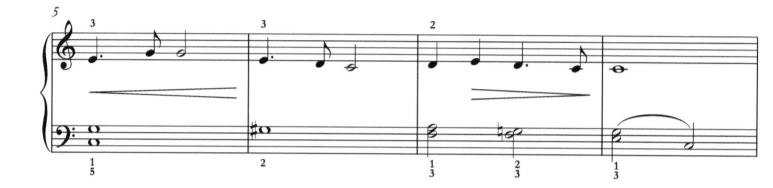

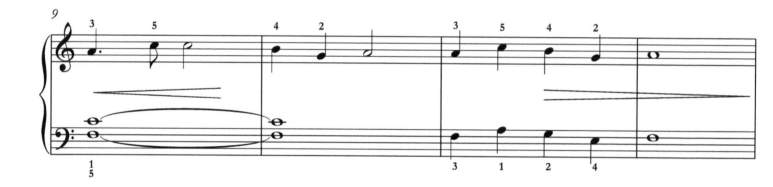

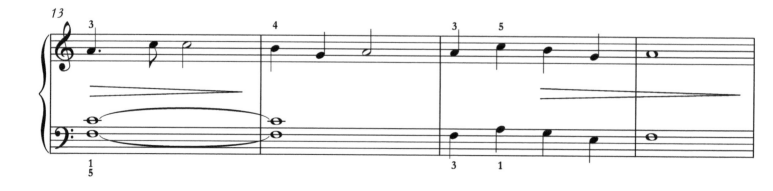

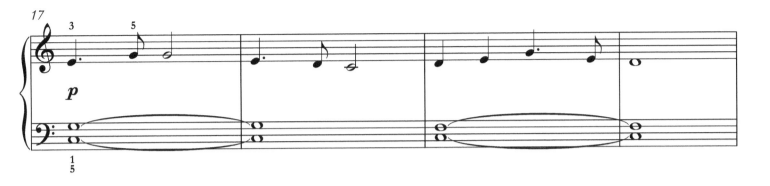

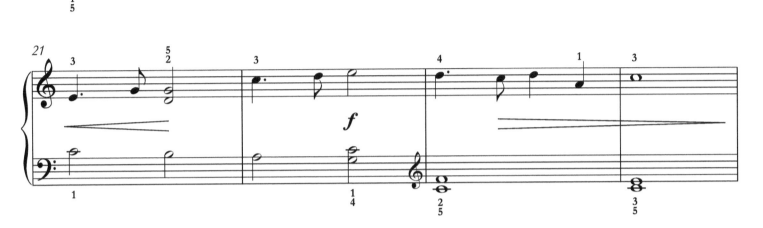

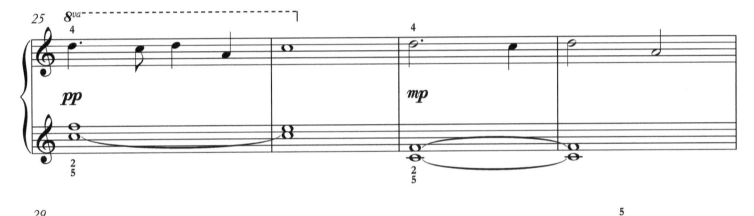

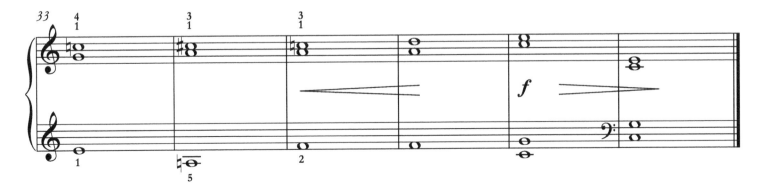

# ETUDE

## Dublin Town

### Gigue

John Thompson

Play one octave
*lower* than written

# SIXTEENTH NOTES

The value of sixteenth notes is HALF that of eighth notes. There are TWO sixteenth notes

to ONE eighth note: and FOUR sixteenth notes to one quarter note:

## John Peel

D'ye ken John Peel with his coat so gay?
D'ye ken John Peel at the break of day?
D'ye ken John Peel when he's far away
With his hounds and his horn in the morning?

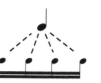

Folk Song

# THE TRILL

# Sweet and Low

Joseph Barnby
1838–1896

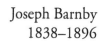

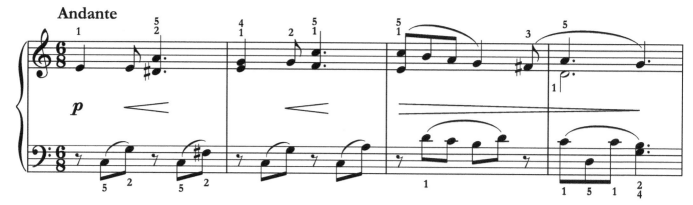

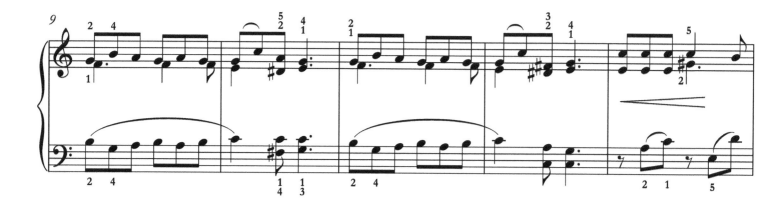

# Under the Leaves

(Sous la feuillée, Op. 29)

Francis Thomé
1850–1909

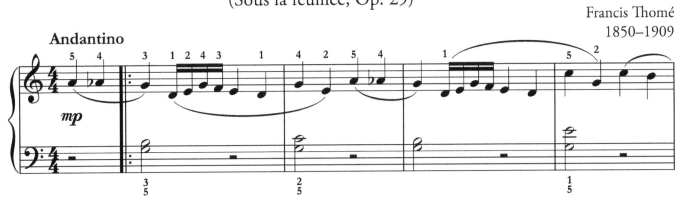

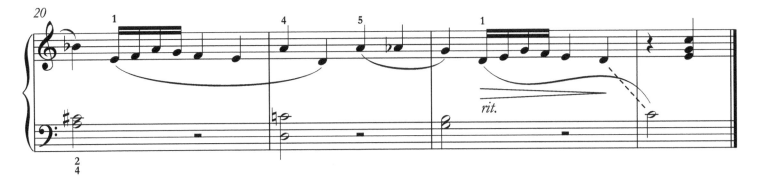

# GLOSSARY

| Signs or Abbreviations | Terms | Meaning |
|---|---|---|
| > | accent | To emphasize or stress a certain note or beat |
| | allegretto | Light and lively |
| | allegro | Fast |
| | andante | Slow |
| | andantino | Slow—but not as slow as *andante* |
| | animato | With animation |
| | arpeggio | In the style of a harp—broken chord |
| | a tempo | Resume original tempo |
| ⊂ | crescendo | A gradual increase in the tone |
| D.C. | Da Capo | Return to the beginning |
| D.C. al Fine | Da Capo al Fine | Return to the beginning and play to *Fine* |
| ⊃ | diminuendo | A gradual decrease in the tone |
| | espressivo | Expressively |
| Fine | Finale | The end |
| *f* | forte | Loud |
| *ff* | fortissimo | Very Loud |
| | largo | Very slowly |
| | legato | Connected, bound together |
| *mf* | mezzo forte | Moderately loud |
| *mp* | mezzo piano | Moderately soft |
| | moderato | At a moderate tempo |
| | molto | Much |
| | nocturne | Night song |
| $8^{va}$⌐ ($8^{vb}$⌐) | octave above (lower) | Play all notes under this sign one octave higher (lower) than written |
| ⌒ | pause, fermata | To hold or pause, according to taste |
| *p* | piano | Softly |
| *pp* | pianissimo | Very softly |
| | poco | Little |
| rit. | ritardando | A gradual slowing of the tempo |
| ♪̄ | sostenuto | Sustained—with singing quality |
| ♪̇ | staccato | Detached |
| | tempo | Time—rate of speed |
| ♪♪♪³ | triplet | Three notes to be played in the time normally given to two |